# Bitcoin

*Sovereignty through mathematics*

KNUT SVANHOLM

Technical Advisor
KALLE ROSENBAUM

SOVEREIGNTY THROUGH MATHEMATICS

Third Edition
Copyright © 2019 Knut Svanholm
All rights reserved.
ISBN: 9781090109910
**Imprint:** Independently published

# DEDICATION

I dedicate this book to my children.
They are scarce, censorship-resistant and a proof of work.

A special thank you to Kalle Rosenbaum, without whom I wouldn't have been half as proud of this book.

# Sovereignty Through Mathematics

## CONTENTS

|    | Foreword | 7 |
|----|----------|---|
| 1  | Everything a trade | 9 |
| 2  | Financial atheism | 15 |
| 3  | The gullible collective | 25 |
| 4  | An immaculate conception | 33 |
| 5  | Proof of work | 41 |
| 6  | Scarcity | 47 |
| 7  | Holding on | 53 |
| 8  | Changing the rules | 63 |
| 9  | Money as an amplifier | 73 |
| 10 | The environment | 83 |
| 11 | A new form of life | 93 |
| 12 | The years ahead | 99 |
|    | Afterthought | 105 |

## Sovereignty Through Mathematics

## FOREWORD

At the time of writing, it is New Year's Day and 2019 has just begun. For once, I have a resolution to live up to. I've promised myself to write a page a day every day this year, until I have something *real* to publish. In June 2018 I published my first book, "Three Minute Reads on Bitcoin - A Year of Thoughts". The book consisted of articles I had published online from May 2017 and up to that point. This time it's different. Instead of a mere collection of articles I intend to write a "proper" book. A book that explains why Bitcoin is the most important invention of our lives. I didn't choose Bitcoin; it chose me. I had been trying to figure out how the world worked under the hood all my life and then this simple idea of absolute scarcity popped up. It had a profound impact on how I view human interaction. Because of my curious nature, I fell deep into the rabbit hole instantly. I decided to educate myself on how this mysterious technology worked and that got me into Austrian economics which expressed very clearly what I had always suspected - that you really can't create value out of thin air. In this book, I will try to explain every aspect of what makes this technology so special, what sets it apart from the abundant shameless copies of it, what's wrong with our current system and what the future might look like. In just two days from the time of writing these words, we'll celebrate the ten year anniversary of the genesis block when the Bitcoin block chain came into being. That block contained a message, a newspaper headline that read: "03/Jan/2009 Chancellor on brink of second bailout for banks". No one knows why Bitcoin's mysterious creator, Satoshi Nakamoto, chose to include this in the genesis block. There is also some debate on whether the genesis block was actually mined on the 3rd of January since the next block wasn't mined until six days later. Somehow Satoshi managed to stay hidden and weave several layers of mystique into the fabric of Bitcoin from the very beginning, which is part of what makes its conception so immaculate. This book aims to strip Bitcoin of its shady cloak and illuminate its true nature. After all, the only thing any person can do about the block chain now is to study it. Note: In this book, Bitcoin *the system* is spelled with a capital B and bitcoin, *the currency* with a small b.

## CHAPTER ONE
## EVERYTHING A TRADE

All human interaction can be defined as trade. Yes, all human interaction. Every time a human being interacts with another, an exchange takes place. In every conversation we have, we exchange information with each other. Even the most trivial information is of some value to the other person. If information didn't have any value to us, we wouldn't talk to each other. Either what the other person says is valuable to us or we find it valuable to give information to them. Oftentimes both. At the core of all human interaction that isn't violent, both parties perceive that they gain some value from it, otherwise the interaction wouldn't have taken place at all. Civilizations begin this way. Two people finding it valuable to interact with each other. That's all it takes. So what constitutes value? What we find valuable is entirely subjective. A comforting hug for example, probably has a different value to a two-year old than it has to a withered army general. Even the most basic action, such as breathing, encapsulates the whole value spectrum. We tend to forget that even a single breath of air can be of immense value to us under the right circumstances. A single breath is worth more than anything on the planet to a desperate free-diver trapped under ice, while worth nothing to a person with a deathwish in clean forest air on a sunny summer day. Value is derived from supply and demand, and demand is always subjective. Supply is not. Since all of our lives are limited by time, time is the ultimate example of a scarce, tradeable resource. We all sell our time. We sell it to others and we sell it to ourselves. Everyone sells their time, either through a product that took them a certain time to produce, or as a service, and services always take time. If you're an employee on a steady payroll, you typically sell eight hours of your day, every day, to your employer. If you're doing something you truly love to do, that eight hour day still belongs to you in a way, since you're doing what you'd probably be doing anyway if you had been forced to do it for free. Sometimes, we sacrifice time in order to acquire something in the future. An education, for instance, gives no immediate reward but can lead to a better-paying, more satisfying job in the future. An investment is basically our future self trading time with our present self at a discount. Once again, every human interaction, viewed as trade. It's rooted in physics. For every action there is an equally large reaction. Trade is at the very core of what we are, and the tools we use to conduct trade matter a lot to the outcome of each transaction. Money is our primary tool for expressing value to each other and if the creation of money is somewhat corrupt or unethical, that rot spreads down throughout society, from top to bottom. Shit flows downhill, as the expression goes. So what is money, or rather, what ought money to be? In order for two persons to interact when a mutual coincidence of needs is absent, a *medium of exchange* is needed in order to execute a transaction. A mutual coincidence of needs might be "You need my three goats and I need your cow", or even "both of us need a hug". In the absence of a physical good or service suitable for a specific transaction, money can fulfill the role of a *medium of exchange*. What most people fail to realise is that the value of money, just as the value of everything else, is entirely subjective. You don't *have* to spend it. The problem with every incarnation of money that mankind has ever tried is that its value always gets diluted over time due to inflation in various forms. Inflation makes traditional money a bad *store of value*, and money needs to be a good *store of value* in order to be a good investment, or in other words, a good substitute for your time and effort over time. Bitcoin tries to solve this by introducing to the world *absolute scarcity*, a concept that mankind has never encountered before. To comprehend what such a discovery means for the future, one needs to understand the fundamentals of what value is, and that we assign a certain value to everything we encounter in life, whether we admit it or not. In short, we assign value to everything we do, value is derived from supply and demand, and supply is *objective* while demand is *subjective*.

Free trade emerges out of human interaction naturally and it is not an idea that was forced upon us at any specific point in time. The idea that markets should be regulated and governed, on the other hand, was. Free trade is just the absence of forceful interference in an interaction between two humans by a third party. There's nothing intrinsically wrong or immoral about an exchange of a good or service. Every objection to this is a byproduct of the current global narrative. A narrative that tells us that the world is divided into different nations and that people in these nations operate under various sets of laws, depending on what jurisdiction they find themselves in. All of these ideas are man-made. No species except humans does this to themselves. Animals do trade, but they don't do politics. Bitcoin, and the idea of truly sound, absolutely scarce money, inevitably makes you question human societal structures in general, and the nature of money in particular. Once you realise that this Pandora's box of an idea can't be closed again by anyone, everything is put into perspective. Once you realise that it is now possible for anyone with a decently sized brain to store any amount of wealth in that brain, or to beam wealth anonymously to any other brain in the world without anyone ever knowing, everything you were ever told about human society is turned on its head. Everything you thought you knew about taxes, social class, capitalism, socialism, economics or even democracy falls apart like a house of cards in a hurricane. It is in fact impossible to comprehend the impact Bitcoin will have on the planet without also understanding basic Austrian economics and what the libertarian worldview stems from.

Imagine growing up in an Amish community. Until your sixteenth birthday you're purposely completely shielded off from the outside world. Information about how the world really works is very limited to you, since internet access, and even TVs and radios, are forbidden within the community. Well, from a certain perspective, we're all Amish. How money really works is never emphasized enough through traditional media or public educational institutions. Most people believe that the monetary system is somehow sound and fair when there's overwhelming evidence to the contrary, all over the globe. Ask yourself, do you remember being taught about the origins of money in school? Me neither. I don't believe that there's some great, global conspiracy behind the fact that the ethics of money creation isn't a school subject, but rather that plain old ignorance is to blame for the lack of such a subject primarily. As soon as their math-skill limit is reached, people seem to stop caring about numbers. The difference between a million and a billion seems lost on a depressingly large part of the world's population. In the chapters ahead we'll explore the pitfalls of central banking, how money pops into existence and how inflation keeps us all on a leash.

## CHAPTER TWO
## FINANCIAL ATHEISM

"Don't trust, verify" is the slogan of a prominent Bitcoin company. The saying represents a sound attitude towards not only Bitcoin, but all human power structures. In order to understand Bitcoin, one must admit that everything in society is man-made. Every civilization, every religion, every constitution and every law is a product of human imagination. It wasn't until as late as the 17th century that the scientific method started to become the dominant practice for describing how the world actually worked. Peer-to-peer review and repeated testing of a hypothesis is still quite a recent human practice. Before this, we were basically just guessing and trusting authorities to a large extent. We still do this today and despite our progress in the last couple of centuries, we still have a long way to go. Our brains are hardwired to follow the leader of the pack. The human brain is born with a plethora of cognitive biases pre-installed and we have to work very hard to overcome them. We evolved to survive in relatively small groups and our brains are thus not really made for seeing the bigger picture. Bitcoin's proof-of-work algorithm is constructed in such a way that it is easy to verify that computational power was sacrificed in order to approve a block of transactions and claim its reward. In this way, no trust in any authority is required as it is relatively trivial to test the validity of a block and the transactions it contains. This is nothing short of a complete reimagining of how human society ought to be governed. The beauty of mathematics governs the Bitcoin system. Everything that ever happens in Bitcoin is open and verifiable to everyone, even to those that are not yet using it.

After the tragic events of 9/11 2001, Sam Harris started writing his book "The End of Faith" which happened to be released around the same time as Richard Dawkins' "The God Delusion", Daniel Dennett's "Breaking the Spell" and Christopher Hitchens' "God Is Not Great: How Religion Poisons Everything". These books kick-started what in hindsight has often been referred to as the *new atheist movement*, even though there has arguably never been anything new about atheism. Atheism must almost certainly have preceded religion since religious ideas require the person holding the idea to believe a certain doctrine or story. Atheism is nothing but the rejection of ways to describe the world that are not verifiable by experimentation. A fly on the wall is probably an atheist by this definition of the word. Atheism is often accused of being just another set of beliefs, but the word itself describes what it is much better - a lack of belief in theistic ideas. It is not a code of conduct or set of rules to live your life by, it is simply the rejection of that which cannot be scientifically verified. Many people, religious people in particular, have a hard time grasping this. If you believe that a supernatural entity created everything in everyone's life, you might not be too comfortable with a word that describes a complete rejection of what you believe created everything, including the very atheist that the word describes. The amount of different religious world views that exist is probably equal to the sum of all religious people on the planet, but all world views that reject these superstitious beliefs require but one word. Atheism is not the opposite of religion but is simply the lack of it.

In 2008, another sub-culture movement of unbelief was born. Let's call it Financial Atheism - the rejection of unverifiable value claims. With the invention of Bitcoin, a way of rejecting fraudulent expressions of a token's value was born. Those of us fortunate enough to have been born in secular countries all enjoy *not* having the ideas of religious demagogues dictating our lives on a daily basis. We can choose which ideas to believe in and which to reject. What we still have very limited means of choosing, however, are the ways in which we express value to each other. We're told to use a system in which we all have a certain number of value tokens assigned to our name, either as a number on a screen or as digits on paper notes. We all live in the collective hallucination that these numbers are somehow legit and that their authenticity is not to be questioned. A Bitcoin balance assigned to a certain Bitcoin address might seem just as questionable to a layman, but if you have a basic understanding of the hashing algorithms and game theory behind it, it's not. At the time of writing, the hash of the latest block on the Bitcoin block chain begins with eighteen zeros in a row. These zeros represent the *Proof of Work* that ensure that this block is valid and that every transaction in it actually happened. If you can grasp the concept of a hashing algorithm, and if you have an intuition about mathematics, you realise the gargantuan amount of calculating effort that went into finding this particular hash. It is simply mind-blowing. To forge a false version of a hash with eighteen zeros in the beginning just wouldn't be economically viable. Of course, you can never actually know that a 51% attack or some other attempt at corrupting the block chain hasn't occurred, but you *can* know that such an attack would require more than half of the network acting against their own economic interest. Bitcoin is not something to *believe* in. You don't need to trust any authority because you can validate the plausibility of its authenticity yourself. It's the financial equivalent of atheism, or unbelief. Satoshi wasn't Jesus. Satoshi was Brian of Nazareth telling his followers to think for themselves.

The first law of thermodynamics, also known as the Law of Conservation of Energy, states that energy cannot be created or destroyed in an isolated system. The second law states that the entropy of any isolated system always increases, and the third law states that the entropy of a system approaches a constant value as the temperature approaches absolute zero. In the Bitcoin network, participants known as miners compete for new Bitcoin in a lottery with very fixed rules. The more hashing power (computing power) a miner contributes to the network, the higher his chances of winning the *block reward*, a specific amount of bitcoins that is halved every four years. The difficulty of this lottery - in other words, the miner's chance of winning it - is re-calibrated every 2016th block, so that the average time it takes to find the next block is always roughly ten minutes. What this system produces is absolute scarcity; the number of bitcoin in existence at any moment in time is always predictable. The more time that passes, the slower the rate of coin issuance and the block reward slowly approaches zero. By the time it does, around the year 2140, the individual miner's incentive to mine for a reward will, at least theoretically, have been replaced by an incentive to collect transaction fees from the participants of the network. Even now, the sum of all fees make up a non-trivial part of the miners' revenue. Yet from a user's point of view the fees are still very low, and as the network scales up using Layer 2 solutions such as the Lightning Network, they're expected to remain low for quite a long time ahead.

Absolute scarcity is a concept that mankind has never encountered before. Arguably, this makes it the first man-made concept to ever be directly linked to the laws of physics. Everything anyone does requires a certain amount of energy. The very word *doing* implies that some kind of movement, some type of energy expenditure, needs to occur. As mentioned earlier, how we value things is entirely subjective. Different actions are of different value to different people. How we value different things is also inevitably linked to the supply of that thing. Had the trapped-under-ice winter diver mentioned in chapter one been equipped with a scuba tank, he probably wouldn't have thought of his next breath as such a precious thing. The price a person is willing to pay for a good - in other words, the sum of one or more person's actions - can be derived from two basic variables: The highly subjective *demand* for the good, and the always-constrained-by-time-and-space *supply* of that same good. Note that if supply is sufficiently limited, there only needs to be a minimal amount of demand for a good for its price to increase. One could argue that no one needs Bitcoin and that therefore Bitcoin would have no intrinsic value. One could also argue that there's no such thing as intrinsic value since demand is always subjective. In any case, there will always be a cost to mine a bitcoin and the more mining power in the network, the higher that cost. This cost, ensured by the Bitcoin network's Proof-Of-Work algorithm, is probably as close to a pure energy cost as the price of a human activity will ever get. Once the mining rig is in place, a simple conversion process follows. Energy in, scarce token out. Should the cost of production exceed the current price of the token, the miner can just choose to not sell, thereby limiting the supply of bitcoins in circulation even more and eventually selling them for other goods, whenever he so sees fit. In this sense, Bitcoin is a battery. Perhaps the best battery ever invented. Storing and moving electrical energy around has always been costly and wasteful. Bitcoin offers a way of converting energy into a small part of a specific number. A mathematical battery, if you will. It is important to remember that it does not convert energy into value directly, but rather electricity into digital scarcity. Digital scarcity which can be used to express value. Energy cannot be created or destroyed in an isolated system as the first law of thermodynamics clearly states. Bitcoin can express how much energy was sacrificed in order to acquire a share of the total sum. You can also acquire bitcoins by buying them, rather than mining them, but in doing so you also spend energy. You somehow acquired the money with which you bought the bitcoins. You, or someone else, sacrificed time and energy somewhere. Bitcoin lets you express that you see that there's a connection between value and scarcity, by letting you sacrifice effort to claim a part of the total sum of them.

The excitement we so-called Bitcoin Maximalists feel about Bitcoin does not come primarily from the enormous gains that those who hopped early onto the freight train have been blessed with. Nor is it because we're "in it for the technology" as can often be heard from opponents. Those of us that preach the near-divinity of this invention do so above all because we see the philosophical impacts of absolute scarcity in a commodity. The idea of a functioning solution to the double-spending problem in computerized money is an achievement that simply can't be ignored. By solving the double-spending problem, Satoshi also made counterfeiting impossible, which in turn makes artificial inflation impossible. The world-changing potential of this invention cannot be understated. Not in the long run. The more you think about it, the more the thought won't give you any peace of mind. If this experiment works, if it's *real*, it will take civilization to the next level. What we don't know is how long this will take. Right now, debates in the Bitcoin space are about bitcoin's functionality as a *medium of exchange* and its potential as a good *store of value*. We might be missing the point. We cannot possibly know if a type of monetary token for which you're completely responsible with no third party protection will ever become a preferred medium of exchange for most transactions. Nor can we know if the price of Bitcoin will follow the hype-cycle path that we all want it to follow, so that it can become the store of value that most maximalists claim that it already is. Maybe we've been focused on the wrong things all along. Maybe Bitcoin's greatest strength is in its functionality as a *unit of account*. After all, this is all that Bitcoin does. If you own 21 bitcoins, you own one-millionth of the world's first absolutely scarce commodity. This might not make you rich overnight, but it just might have something to do with the opportunities available to your great-great grandchildren.

Throughout history, whenever a prehistoric human tribe invented ceremonial burial, that tribe began to expand rapidly. Why? Because as soon as you invent belief in an afterlife, you also introduce the idea of self-sacrifice on a larger scale. People that held these beliefs were much easier for a despot to manipulate and send into battle with neighbouring tribes. Religious leaders can use people's fears and superstitions to have them commit all sorts of atrocities to their fellow man and they still do so today. Belief in a "greater good" can be the most destructive idea that can pop up in a human mind. The Nazis of World War II Germany believed that exterminating jews was for the "greater good" of their nation's gene pool. Belief in noble causes often comes with unintended side effects which can have disastrous consequences. Religious leaders, political leaders, and other power-hungry sociopaths are responsible for the greatest crimes against humanity ever committed - namely, wars. We Europeans often question the Second Amendment to the United States Constitution, which protects the right to bear arms, whenever a tragic school shooting occurs on the other side of the Atlantic. What everyone seems to forget is that less than a hundred years ago, Europe was at war with itself because its citizens had given too much power to their so-called leaders. The Nazis came to power in a democracy - never forget that. Our individual rights weren't *given* to us by our leaders; we were born with them. Our leaders can't *give* us anything; they can only force us to behave in certain ways. If we truly want to be in charge of our lives we need to find the tools necessary to circumvent the bullshit ourselves.

## CHAPTER THREE
## THE GULLIBLE COLLECTIVE

We humans are biased by nature. Everything we think we know is distorted in one way or another by our cognitive shortcomings. The human brain has been forced to evolve and adapt to whatever environment it found itself in over millennia. Having a brain that is capable of setting aside personal aims for the sake of the collective has proven to be advantageous for the evolution of our species as a whole. The same is true for every other social life-form. However, to let these parts of our brains guide our political judgement can lead to disastrous results in the long run. Not because of bad intentions but for the simple fact that a few individuals will always thrive by playing every political system for personal gains. From an evolutionary perspective, an army of ay-sayers and martyrs, regardless of whether we're talking about an army of humans or an army of ants or bacteria, has an advantage over a less disciplined one. From an individual's evolutionary perspective though, it is better to *appear* like you're a martyr but to run and hide when the actual battle happens. This at least partly explains the high percentage of sociopaths in leadership positions all over the world. If you can appear to act for the good of the collective but dupe your way into more and more power behind people's backs, you're more likely to succeed than someone playing a fair game.

The story of banking and fiat currency is a story about collective madness. Historically, rulers have tricked people into killing each other through the promise of an after-life. Through central banking, the rulers of the world wars could trick people into building armies for them by printing more money. This is seldom mentioned in history classes because it still goes on today, on a massive scale. Inflation might no longer be paying tank-factory workers, but it is the main mechanism that funnels wealth into the pockets of the super rich and away from everyone else. Inflation is the mechanism that hinders us from transporting the value of our labour through time. It makes us avoid real long term thinking. We hardly ever consider this a problem, because none of us has ever experienced an alternative to it. Money is still vastly misunderstood by the lion's share of the world's population. In most parts of the world, banks do something called fractional reserve lending. This means that they lend out money that they don't have. Conjuring up new money out of thin air and handing it out to their customers as loans. Loans which have to be paid back with interest. Interest that can't be paid back with thin air, but has to be paid with so called real money. Real money, of which there isn't enough around to pay back all the loans, so that a constant need for new credit becomes a crucial part of the entire system. Not to mention central banks that do the same and worse to governments. We're so used to it by now that every country is expected to have a national debt. All but a handful of ridiculously rich ones do. National debts are also loans which have to be paid back with interest backed by nothing. Think about that. Your taxes are paying someone else's interest. Your tax money is not paying for your grandmother's bypass operation, it is paying interest to a central bank.

When the ideas of the catholic church ruled Europe, people who didn't believe in God were few and very seldomly outspoken. They had good reason for this, since belief in God was virtually mandatory throughout society. Ever since 1971, when famously dishonest american president Richard Nixon cut the last string that tied the US Dollar to gold, our conception of what the world economy is, and ought to be has been skewed by an utterly corrupt system. We're led to believe that we're all supposed to work longer and longer days in order to spend more and more and bury ourselves in more and more debt to keep the machine running. We're duped into thinking that buying a new car every other year is somehow good for the environment. That bringing a cotton bag to the grocery store will save the planet. Stores manipulate us all the time through advertising and product placement, but we're led to believe that if we can be "climate smart" we're behaving responsibly. Somehow, our gross domestic product is supposed to increase infinitely while politicians will save us from ourselves through carbon taxes. Fortunately for us, and unfortunately for them, there now exists a way for unbelievers of this narrative, to opt out. Life finds a way, as Jeff Goldblum once so famously put it.

Collectivism has ruined many societies. Those of us fortunate enough to live in liberal democracies tend to forget that even democracy is an involuntary system. It's often referred to as the "worst form of government except all others that have been tried", but the system itself is very rarely criticized. We're so used to being governed that not having a leader seems preposterous to most of us. Still, we pay our taxes and an enormous cut of the fruit of our labour goes to a third party via inflation and the taxation of every good and service imaginable. Institutions, once in place, tend to always favor their own survival just as much as any other living thing does. People employed in the public sector are unlikely to vote against policies that threaten their livelihood. This is a bigger problem than we realise because it's subtle and takes a long time, but every democracy is headed in the same direction. A bigger state, a more complicated system and fewer individual freedoms. Long term, it seems that all of our systems tend to favor those who know how to play that system and not those who contribute the most value to their fellow man. Proponents of socialist policies often claim that failed socialist states "weren't really socialist" or that "that wasn't really socialism". What most people fail to realise is that we've never tried *real capitalism* since we've always used more or less inflationary currencies. This might very well be the most skewed narrative of our era. We're all experiencing real, albeit disguised, socialism every single day. True free market capitalism is what we haven't experienced yet and it might turn out to be a very different thing than what we're told to believe that it is, by almost all mainstream media.

The validity of the classic right-left scale describing political viewpoints has been debated a lot lately and alternative scales, like GAL-TAN, the one with an additional Y-axis describing more or less authoritarian tendencies, are popping up in various contexts around the web. After the birth of Bitcoin, there's a new way to see this. Imagine an origo, a zero point, and a vector pointing to the left of that. *All* politics are arguably on the left because *all* policies need to be funded by taxes and taxation can be viewed as theft. Taxation can be viewed as theft because at its core, it's involuntary. If a person refuses to pay his taxes, there is a threat of violence lurking in the background. Not to mention inflation, which Milton Friedman so elegantly described as "taxation without legislation". What you do with the portion of your wealth that you have in bitcoin is another matter altogether. If you take sufficient precautionary privacy measures and you know what you're doing, your business in bitcoin is beyond politics all together. With the introduction of the Lightning Network and other privacy improving features, it is now impossible for any third party to confiscate your money, or even know that you have it for that matter. This changes the political landscape of every nation on Earth. Bitcoin is much less confiscatable than gold and other scarce assets, which makes it a much better tool for hedging against nation states. In this sense, Bitcoin obsoletes borders. You can cross any border on Earth with any amount of bitcoins *in your head*. Think about that. Your bitcoins exist in every country simultaneously. Any imposed limit on how much money you can carry from one nation to the other is now made obsolete by beautiful mathematics. Bitcoin is sometimes referred to as a "virtual currency". This is a very inaccurate description. Bitcoin is just mathematics, and mathematics is just about the most real thing there is. There's nothing virtual about it. Counterintuitive to some, but real nonetheless.

The complexity of human societal hierarchies and power structures are described perfectly in a classic children's book. "The Emperor's New Clothes", by Hans Christian Andersen. See the world as the kid that points out that the king is naked in the tale, and everything starts to make sense. Everything in human society is man-made. Nations, leaders, laws, political systems. They're all castles in the air with nothing but a lurking threat of violence to back them up. Bitcoin is a different beast all together. It enables every individual to verify the validity of the system at all times. If you really think about it, morality is easy. Don't hurt other people and don't steal other people's stuff. That's the basic premise. Humans have but two ways of resolving conflict, conversation and violence, and in this sense, to hurt someone can only mean physical violence. This is why free speech is so important and why you should defend people's right to speak their mind above everything else. It's not about being able to express yourself, it's about your right to hear every side of every argument and thus not have to resort to violence should a conflict of interests occur. You can't limit free speech with just more speech, there's always a threat of violence behind the limitations. Code, which both Bitcoin and the internet are entirely made up of, *is speech*. Any limitations or regulations that your government implements in regard to Bitcoin is not only a display of Bitcoin's censorship resistance, but also a test of your government's stance on freedom of expression. A restriction on Bitcoin use is a restriction on free speech. Remember that the only alternative to speech that anyone has, is violence. Code is a language, mathematics is a language and money is a linguistic tool. A linguistic tool we use as a means of expressing value to each other and as a way to transport value through space and time. Any restrictions or regulations regarding how you can express value, i.e. making it impossible to buy bitcoins with your credit card, proves that the money you have in your bank account is not really yours. When people realise this, the demand for Bitcoin goes *up*, not down. If you know what you're doing, there's no need to fear the regulators. They, on the other hand, have good reason to fear an invention that shamelessly breaks their spell.

# CHAPTER FOUR
# AN IMMACULATE CONCEPTION

Some concepts in nature are harder for us humans to understand than others. How complex things can emerge out of simpler ones is one of those concepts. A termite colony for instance, has a complex cooling system in its lower levels. No single termite knows how it works. Completely unaware of the end results they build complex mounds and nests, shelter tubes to protect their paths, and networks of subterranean tunnels to connect their dirt cities. Everything seems organized and designed but it is not. Evolution has equipped the termite with a pheromone receptor that tells the termite what task he ought to engage himself in, by simply counting the amount of neighboring termites doing the same thing. If there's a surplus of workers in an area, nearby termites become warriors and so on.

Complex structures emerge from simple rules. The fractal patterns found all around nature is another example. Fractals look complex but in reality they're not. They're basically algorithms. The same pattern, repeated over and over again with a slightly modified starting point. The human brain is an excellent example of a complex thing that evolved out of simpler things and we humans still have a hard time accepting that it wasn't designed. Religions, which themselves are emergent systems spawned out of human interaction, have come up with a plethora of explanations for how we came to be. All sorts of wild origin stories have been more widely accepted than the simple explanation that our complexities just emerged out of simpler things following a set of rules that nature itself provided our world with.

Complex systems emerge out of human interactions all the time. The phone in your pocket is the result of a century of mostly free global market competition, and no single human could ever have come up with the entire thing. The device, together with its internet connection, is capable of a lot more than the sum of its individual parts. A pocket-sized gadget that can grant instant access to almost all of the world's literature, music and film, that fits in your pocket was an unthinkable science fiction a mere twenty years ago. Bitcoin, first described in Satoshi Nakamoto's white paper ten years before these words were written, was designed to be decentralized but it wasn't until years later that the network started to show actual proof of this. Sound money, or absolute digital scarcity, emerged out of the network not only because of its technical design. How Bitcoin's first ten years actually unfolded played a huge part in how true decentralization could emerge and this is also the main reason as to why the experiment can not be replicated. Scarcity on the internet could only be invented once. Satoshi's disappearance was Bitcoin's first step towards true decentralization. No marketing whatsoever and the randomness of who hopped onto the train first, were the steps that followed. Bitcoin truly had an immaculate conception. The network has shown a remarkable resistance to change over the last few years especially, and its current state might be its last incarnation given the size of the network and the 95% agreement threshold in its consensus rules. It might never change again. In that case, an entirely new, complex life form will have emerged out of a simple set of rules. Even if small upgrades are implemented in the future, the 21 million coin supply cap is set in stone forever. Bitcoin is not for humans to have opinions about, it exists regardless of what anyone thinks about it, and it ought to be studied rather than discussed. We don't know what true scarcity and a truly global, anonymous free market will do to our species yet, but we are about to find out. It is naive to think otherwise. Various futurists and doomsday prophets have been focused on the dangers of the impending *general artificial intelligence singularity* lately, warning us about the point of no return, whereupon an artificial intelligence will be able to improve itself faster than any human could. Such a scenario could, as news anchor Ron Burgundy would have put it, escalate quickly. This may or may not be of real concern to us but meanwhile, right under our noses, another type of unstoppable digital life has emerged and it is already changing the behaviour and preferences of millions of people around the globe. This is probably bad news for big corporations and governments but good news for the little guy looking for a little freedom. At least that's what those of us who lean towards the ideas of the Austrian school of economics believe. This time around, we will find out whether this is the case or not. No one knows what it will lead to and what new truths will emerge out of this new reality.

Unlike the termite we humans are able to experience the grandeur of our progress. We can look in awe at the Sistine Chapel or the pyramids, and we can delve into the technicalities and brief history of Bitcoin and discover new ways of thinking about value along the way. Money is the language in which we express value to each other through space and time. Now that language is spoken by computers. Value expressed in this language can't be diluted through inflation or counterfeiting any longer. It is a language that is borderless, permissionless, peer-to-peer, anonymous if you have the skills, unreplicable, completely scarce, non-dilutable, unchangeable, untouchable, undeniable, fungible and free for everyone on Earth to use. It is a language for the future and it emerged out of a specific set of events in the past. All languages are examples of complex systems emerging out of simpler things, and Bitcoin evolved just as organically as any other human language did.

Decentralization is hard to achieve. Really hard. When it comes to claims of decentralization, a "don't trust, verify" -approach to the validity of such claims will help you filter out the noise. So how can the validity of Bitcoin's decentralization be verified? It's a tricky question, because decentralization is not a binary thing, like life or death, but rather a very difficult concept to define. However, the most fundamental concepts in Bitcoin, like the 21 million cap on coin issuance or the ten minute block interval as a result of the difficulty adjustment and the Proof of Work algorithm, has not changed since very early on in the history of the network. This lack of change, which is arguably Bitcoin's biggest strength, has been achieved through the consensus rules, which define what the block chain is. Some special mechanisms (for example BIP9) are sometimes used to deploy changes of the consensus rules. These mechanisms use a threshold when counting blocks that signal for a certain upgrade. For example, the upgrade "Segregated Witness" activated in a node when 95% or more of the blocks in a retarget period signalled support. Bitcoin has displayed a remarkable immutability through the years and it is highly unlikely that this would have been the case if the game-theoretical mechanisms that enable its decentralized governance model hadn't worked, given the many incentives to cheat that always seem to corrupt monetary systems. In other words, the longer the system seems to be working, the higher the likelihood that it actually does.

Satoshi set in stone the length of the *halving period*, a very important aspect of Bitcoin's issuance schedule and initial distribution. During the first four years of Bitcoin's existence, fifty new coins were issued every ten minutes up until the first *block reward halving* four years later. Every four years this reward is halved, so that the issuance rate goes down by fifty percent. This effectively means that half of all the bitcoins that would ever exist were mined during the first four years of the network's life, one fourth during its next four years and so on. At the time of writing we're a little more than a year from the third halving. After that, only 6.25

bitcoins will be minted every ten minutes as opposed to 50, which was the initial rate. What this seems to do is to create hype-cycles for Bitcoin's adoption. Every time the price of bitcoin booms and then busts down to a level above where it started, a hype-cycle takes place. Bitcoin had no marketing whatsoever so awareness of it had to spread by some other mechanism. When a bull run begins, people start talking about it which leads to even more people buying due to *Fear Of Missing Out* or FOMO, which inevitably makes the price rise even more rapidly. This leads to more FOMO and on and on the bull market goes until it suddenly ends and the price crashes down to somewhere around, or slightly above, the level it was at before the bull run started. Unlike what is true for most other assets, bitcoin never really crashes all the way. Why? Because every time a hype-cycle occurs some more people learn about Bitcoin's fundamentals and manage to resist the urge to sell, even when almost all hope seems lost. They understand that these bull markets are a reoccurring thing due to the nature of the protocol. These cycles create new waves of evangelists who start promoting Bitcoin simply because of what they stand to gain from a price increase. In a sense, the protocol itself pays for its own promotion in this way. This organic marketing creates a lot of noise and confusion too, as a lot of people who don't seem to understand how Bitcoin works often are very outspoken about it despite their lack of knowledge. Red herrings, such as altcoins and Bitcoin forks, are then weeded out naturally during bear markets. Every time a bull market happens, a new generation of Bitcoiners is born. The four year period between halvings seems to serve a deliberate purpose. Satoshi could just as well have programmed a smooth issuance curve into the Bitcoin protocol but he didn't. As events unfold, it seems that he had good reason for this since these hype-cycles provide a very effective on-boarding mechanism and they seem to be linked to the halvings. They certainly make bitcoin volatile but remember that in this early stage, the volatility is needed in order for these hype-cycles to happen. Later on, when Bitcoin's stock-to-flow ratio is higher, the seas will calm and its volatility level will go down. In truth, it already has. The latest almost 80% price drop was far from the worst we've seen in bitcoin. This technology is still in its infancy and it is very likely that we'll see a lot more of this volatility before mainstream adoption, or *hyperbitcoinisation*, truly happens.

## CHAPTER FIVE
## PROOF OF WORK

Zoom out of time for a while and imagine how the antlers of a magnificent moose buck evolved into being. The main purpose of big antlers in nature is believed to be a way for the buck to impress potential mates. They're somewhat akin to the feathers of a peacock, or the shroud of any male bird for that matter. The animal is trying to signal that it can thrive in its environment despite its enormous appendage. It's there to tell the potential mate that this specific specimen will bring her strong, healthy offspring. These are all evolutionary metaphors of course, the animal itself is probably unaware of signalling anything. For such antlers to evolve into being, a whole lot of moose will have to die early, or at least not get a chance to reproduce, over thousands of generations. In other words, a lot of resources need to be wasted. All of this for the animal to prove its value to potential spouses. Therefore, from the surviving moose's point of view, the aforementioned resources were sacrificed rather than wasted.

The Proof of Work algorithm in Bitcoin does a similar thing. It enables miners to sacrifice a lot of electricity, a real world resource, to find a certain number and thereby proving that they had to commit a lot of time and effort to do this. Time, by the way, is the scarcest of all resources. Because of all this, a Bitcoin miner is very reluctant to sell bitcoins at a net loss. The electricity has already been used when the bitcoins pop into existence and the miner has no other means of getting his money back than by selling the bitcoins for more than the cost of the electricity it took to produce them. This is assuming that the mining rig itself has already been paid for. Proof of Work is a way of converting computing power into money in a sense. Yes, these rigs consume a lot of energy, but the energy consumed correlates directly to the actual value of the created token. Any decrease in the energy expenditure would also lead to a decrease in the value of the token. Not necessarily the price but the *actual value*. This is the main reason mining algorithms can't be less resource consuming or more energy efficient. "Wasting" energy is the whole point. No "waste", no proof of commitment.

# Bitcoin

The fundamental principles of Bitcoin were set in stone in 2008 and block #0, the so-called *genesis block*, was mined in January, 2009. In Bitcoin, a block of transactions is created every ten minutes. In its first four years of existence, these blocks included a 50 bitcoin block reward, given to the miner who found the block. Every four years, this reward is halved so that the maximum number of bitcoins that can ever be claimed can never exceed just short of 21 million. Every 2016th block, or roughly every two weeks, the difficulty of finding a new block is re-calibrated so that a block will be found every ten minutes on average. The value of this feature, and the impact it has on coin issuance, is often understated. It is one of the features of Bitcoin that separates it from gold and other assets in one of the most subtle, yet most powerful ways. When the price of gold or silver or oil or any other asset goes up, producing that asset becomes more profitable and more resources are allocated to produce more of it, faster. This in turn evens out the price as the total supply of said asset increases. Gold has been able to maintain or increase its value long term over time because of its high stock-to-flow ratio. Stock refers to the supply of an asset currently available on the market. Flow refers to the amount added to the stock per time unit. The bigger the stock in relation to the flow, the less of an impact on the total supply an increase in the price of a specific asset has. In Bitcoin, a price increase has virtually no impact at all on the coin issuance rate, or flow, since the difficulty of finding the next block in the chain is constantly being optimized for a strict issuance schedule. No other asset has ever behaved like this and we are yet to find out what impact its existence will have on the world economy.

So how does one mine a block in the Bitcoin block chain? In short, the mining process goes something like this. Every active node in the Bitcoin network stores a copy of the *mempool*, which contains all bitcoin transactions that haven't been confirmed yet. The miner puts as many transactions as the block size allows into the block, usually selecting those with the highest fee first. He then adds a random number, called a *nonce*, and produces a hash of the entire thing using the SHA-256 hashing algorithm. A hashing algorithm turns data into a string of numbers. If the resulting hash begins with a specific number of zeros decided by the current difficulty of the network, the miner wins the block reward, collects all the fees and gets to put the block on the block chain. The beauty of the system is that it is trivial for the nodes in the network to verify the block so that no double spending can occur, but it's near impossible to forge a fake hash since the probability of finding one that begins with as many zeros as the difficulty of the Bitcoin network demands is extremely low. To a layman's eye a hash beginning with a bunch of zeros just looks like a random number, but a person who understands the mathematics behind it sees a different thing. The zeros act as proof of an enormous commitment to trying out different nonces and trying to find a perfect match. If you're able to understand these huge numbers you quickly realise that this number must have been created by devoting computing power to doing just that, on an absolutely massive scale. The proof is in those zeros. If you compare just the hash rate of the top five so-called cryptocurrencies, it is obvious that Bitcoin is on a different level security-wise. From a hash rate to security perspective, the Ethereum block chain is about five times as ineffective and the Litecoin block chain about ten times as ineffective as the Bitcoin block chain at the time of writing (Source: howmanyconfs.com). This in addition to the obviously more centralized nature of these "alternatives".

Some of the futurists and doomsday prophets mentioned in chapter four as the people most likely to warn us about the dangers of the impending Artificial Intelligence singularity, believe that we already live in a simulated reality. The main argument for this world view is that since simulations and computer graphics seem to be getting better at an ever accelerating rate, we can't really know if we already live in a simulation or not. To put it another way, we simply have no way of knowing if we live in The Matrix or if our perceived reality is all there is. A really mind-blowing counter argument to this theory is that Bitcoin's Proof of Work algorithm would eventually slow down the simulation since Proof of Work is verifiable and can't be simulated itself. Computing power would have to be sacrificed by some entity somewhere, regardless. One question remains though. Can the inhabitants of a simulated reality actually feel or measure a slowdown of the very simulation they live in?

## CHAPTER SIX
## SCARCITY

What makes a commodity scarce? What is scarcity in the first place? What other properties can be deducted from an object's scarcity? How are scarcity, energy, time and value connected? Scarcity might seem easy to describe on the surface, but in reality it's not. Not when you take infinity into account. Infinity is a concept that has puzzled the human mind for as long as it has been able to imagine it. If it ever has. It is a very abstract concept and it's always linked to time, simply because even imagining an infinite number would take an infinite amount of time. If we truly live in an infinite universe, scarcity cannot exist. If something exists in an infinite universe, an infinite number of copies of this something must also exist, since the probability of this being true would also be infinite in an infinite universe. Therefore, scarcity must always be defined within a set framework. No frame, no scarcity.

Think of it this way. The most expensive artwork ever sold at the time of writing was the "Salvator Mundi", painted by Leonardo da Vinci. It's not even a particularly beautiful painting, so why the high price? Because Da Vinci originals are scarce. A poster of the painting isn't expensive at all but the original will cost you at least 450 million US Dollars. All because we agree to frame its scarcity around the notion that it is a Da Vinci original, of which under twenty exist today. Historically, scarcity has always been framed around real world limits to the supply of a good. Most of the great thinkers of the Austrian school of economics from the twentieth century believed that the value of a monetary good arises from its scarcity and that scarcity is always connected to the real world availability of that good. Most of them believed that a gold standard would be the hardest form of money that we would ever see, and the closest thing to an absolutely scarce resource as we would ever know.

In the late 90's, the cryptographers that laid the groundwork for what would become Bitcoin reimagined scarcity as anything with an unforgeable costliness. This mindset is key to understanding the connection between scarcity and value. Anything can be viewed as scarce if it's sufficiently hard to produce and hard to fake the production cost of. In other words, easy to verify the validity of. The zeros in the beginning of a hashed Bitcoin block are the proof-of-work that proves that the created coins in that block were costly to produce. People who promote the idea that the mining algorithm used to produce bitcoin could be more environmentally friendly or streamlined are either deliberately lying or missing the point. The energy expenditure is the very thing that gives the token its value because it provides proof to the network that enough computing power was sacrificed in order to keep the network sufficiently decentralized and thus resistant to change. Easy to verify is the flipside of the unforgeable costliness coin. The validity of a Bitcoin block is very easy to verify, since all you need to do is look at the hash of it, make sure the block is part of the strongest chain, and that it conforms to all consensus rules. In order to check that a gold bar is real or not, you probably need to trust a third party. Fiat money often comes with a plethora of water stamps, holograms and metal stripes so in a sense, they're hard to forge. What you cannot know about a fiat currency at any given moment though, is how much of it there is in circulation. What you *do* know is that they're *not* scarce.

Bitcoin provides us with absolute scarcity, for the first time in human history. It is a remarkable breakthrough.

Even though you can't make jewellery or anything else out of bitcoins, their total supply is fixed. After the year 2140, after the last bitcoin has been mined, the total amount of bitcoins in circulation can only go down. This limited supply is what the gold standards of the past were there for in the first place. Bitcoin's supply is much more limited than that of gold, however, since they will be lost as time goes by. Since the supply is so limited it doesn't matter what the current demand is. The potential upside to its value is literally limitless due to this relationship between supply and demand. The "backing" that other currencies have is only there to ensure people that the currency will keep its value over time and the only way of ensuring this is to limit the supply. Bitcoin does this better than any other thing before it. Leonardo da Vinci's original paintings are extremely valuable because of Leonardo's brand name and the fact that there's only about 13 of them left. One day there'll be less than one left. The same is true for bitcoin.

Scarcity on the internet was long believed to be an impossible invention and it took a multi-talented genius such as Satoshi Nakamoto to figure out all the different parts that make Bitcoin so much more than the sum of them. His disappearance from the project was one such part, maybe the most important one. The thing about computerized scarcity is that it was a one time invention. Once it was invented, the invention could not be recreated. That's just the nature of data. Computers are designed to be able to replicate any data set any number of times. This is true for every piece of code there is and digital scarcity needed to be framed somehow to work. Bitcoin's consensus rules provided such a frame. Bitcoin certainly seems to provide true digital scarcity and if the game theoretical theories that it builds on are correct, its promise of an ever increasing value will be a self-fulfilling prophecy.

In 2018, the inflation rate of the Venezuelan Bolivar was a staggering 80,000%. Hugo Chavez, and his successor Nicolas Maduro, effectively killed the Venezuelan economy with Socialism. It has happened before—and sadly, it is likely to happen again. The main problem with Socialism is not that people aren't incentivized to work in socialist countries. On the contrary, hungry people under the threat of violence tend to work harder than most. The problem with State-owned production is that there is no free market price mechanism to reflect the true demand for goods, and therefore, no way of knowing how much supply the State should produce. Everything is in constant surplus or shortage—often the latter, as the empty supermarket shelves in Venezuela depressingly attest. Chavez and Maduro attempted to rescue the country's economy by printing more money—which simply does not work.

Their true motives for printing money are, of course, questionable given that it depreciated the value of Bolivar bills to less than that of toilet paper. As mentioned in earlier chapters, inflation is the greatest hidden threat to themselves that humans have ever created. A few hundred years ago, the Catholic Church held the lion's share of political power throughout Europe. Today, power mostly resides with nation-states in collusion with multinational corporations. The separation of Church and State triggered the migration of power from the former to the latter, emancipating many citizens in the process. Still, places like Venezuela are sad proof that "the people" are still not in power in many self-proclaimed democracies—if in any, for that matter. Another separation will have to take place first: The separation of money and State. We, the people of planet Earth, now have the means at our disposal for this separation to take place. Whether we use them or not will determine how emancipated and independent our children can and will be in the future.

## CHAPTER SEVEN
## HOLDING ON

In the old days, we Scandinavians had to save in order to prepare for the long winter. We chopped wood and salted meat in order to survive. In our current age of consumerism, however, we've forgotten all that and we pilgrim to the shopping malls as much as everyone else. No one seems to even have a savings account anymore. Interest rates are low and we're told to borrow and spend as much as we can. We're bombarded with advertising for loans, mortgages, and financial services on a daily basis. Why? Because of our inability to understand the nature of money and its mechanics. Inflation is the underlying force that makes us squander rather than save. Inflation hinders us from reaping the fruits of our labour whenever we so think fit, and it makes that very fruit rot. Bitcoin reverses the rotting process and provides us with a means of transporting the value of our labour not only through space but also through time.

The *Stanford Marshmallow Experiments* was a series of studies on delayed gratification conducted in the late 1960s and early 1970s. In the experiments, children were given a marshmallow or a cookie and were told that they would receive an additional one if they could control their urges and not touch the first one for fifteen minutes. Follow-up studies found that the kids that were able to resist the temptation of the first cookie tended to score better on SAT tests, have lower BMIs and higher incomes than their less-disciplined counterparts. Investing in your future self—in other words, resisting present temptation by delaying gratification—is the most effective skill you can cultivate for a brighter future. You reap what you sow. This can be described as having a *low time preference*. Having a low time preference is a fundamental factor in the economic success of any human endeavor. Not trying to catch fish with your hands for a couple of days in order to construct a rod or net when on a deserted island, might make you hungry during those sacrificed days but will provide a better chance of catching fish in the future. Likewise, learning new skills now might lead to a higher salary in the future. Unfortunately, our current monetary system distorts our perceptions and incentives and favors those with higher time preference—those that spend rather than save. We're at a different point in history than the above-mentioned marooned fisherman. Give a man a fish and feed him for a day, teach a man to fish and feed him for a lifetime, the saying goes. The ultimate goal should be to teach mankind to teach itself how to fish. What our current paradigm endorses is "give a man enough distractions, and he will stop thinking about finding better ways to support his loved ones and will succumb to whatever narrative you fill his head with, to make him work for you through taxes and inflation instead of for himself."

In Bitcoin, people with a low time preference win. If you can resist the urge to sell, you will be rewarded in the future. The Bitcoin community refers to not selling as HODLing, which originated when a bitcointalk.org forumer named GameKyuubi misspelled the word "holding" in a now-famous post titled I AM HODLING. The post became one of the Bitcoin community's most prominent memes and a battle cry to resist the urge to sell during bear markets. Bitcoiners who have decided to never sell most or all of their holdings are referred to as *HODLers of last resort*. This term is not to be confused with the central banking term *lender of last resort*. The yearly highs in the price of

Bitcoin are arguably less interesting than the yearly lows, which are practically decided by these *HODLers of last resort*. Considering its limited supply, all that Bitcoin needs to keep rising in price over the medium and long term are these people. Adoption and other metrics of measuring the success of Bitcoin are all dwarfed by the currency's remarkable rise in value since its inception. The price has multiplied upward by ten approximately every three years. The best guarantee we have that it will keep doing this is Bitcoin's limited supply combined with the *HODLers of last resort*.

In the Bitcoin space, and even more so in the cryptocurrency space on the whole, there's a lot of talk about usage and adoption. We're shown metrics of trading volumes and merchant acceptance and we're led to believe that these correlate with the short and long term value in one way or another. While there may be truth in some of these theories, the most basic function of a deflationary asset is overlooked and rarely mentioned—the elephant in the room, so to speak. The best use for a commodity as scarce as Bitcoin is not to spend it, or even to trade it, but to save it and hold it for as long as you can. By doing so, you limit the number of coins in circulation. The more people that do this, the harder it will be to come by and the higher its price will be. Nothing on Earth is as scarce as Bitcoin. Nothing is as irreplicable, as immutable, and at the same time as portable as Bitcoin. Its unique history and resistance to change has already proven this over and over. Its absolute scarcity is what gives Bitcoin its value, and ironically enough, this seems to be the hardest thing for people to understand about it. What if everyone in the network became a HODLer and decided to never sell, wouldn't the network just slowly come to a halt? Not at all. Everyone has a price. Few would resist selling some of their bitcoins if it could buy them a small city. There are price levels for each HODLer where reallocating financially may be a wise thing to do. A bitcoin is also very divisible: The smallest unit, *satoshi,* sometimes referred to as a *sat,* is one-hundred millionth of a bitcoin. Even smaller units are made possible with the introduction of the Lightning Network, albeit not in the actual Bitcoin block chain. Together, this enables bitcoins to be highly saleable even at astronomical price levels.

What *not* having sound money has done to us is simply unfathomable. Imagine every person on Earth knowing that every transaction they'll ever make will have a real impact on their future prosperity. We're so used to inflationary currencies that most people don't even realise *why* sound money is important. We're so used to having a large cut of our income silently taken away from us that we don't even realise how much of our day we spend working for someone else. Wars are funded by inflation. Try to imagine how many man-hours were put in by people that didn't realise they were actually working for a war machine funded by a corrupt currency during World War II. Every time you use a fiat currency you legitimize counterfeiting. Every time you use Bitcoin you promote *sound money*. In fact, every time you *don't* use your bitcoins but save them instead, you promote sound money, because sound money increases in value when the total number of coins in circulation is limited. It all sounds a bit magic and far-fetched, doesn't it? Increased value over time, no matter what happens? Well, that is why many of us so-called Bitcoin Maximalists are so excited that we put our career at risk for this technology. Once you realise what Bitcoin is and what it will do for the world, there is no way of un-realising it. It really is mind-blowing.

At the beginning of time-that-actually-*is*-money—in other words, around 2009—Bitcoin was mostly considered a toy for the cypherpunk movement. As its price started to grow rapidly, a small group of early investors became very wealthy, which in turn spawned a media hype around the phenomenon. The mainstream media remained largely skeptical, portraying Bitcoin as a pyramid scheme, a tulip craze or a bubble at best. Most journalists simply couldn't understand how an asset seemingly created out of thin air could have any long-term relevance. Some were frustrated because they thought that they'd missed the train. Many still do. In a world where companies like Google, Facebook and Amazon can rise from zero to world dominance in a decade, people tried to find the Next Big Thing—the next Bitcoin. This attracted charlatans and scammers to the field who launched hundreds of altcoins claiming to someday be technically superior, faster, or more privacy-focused. What the snake-oil salespeople omitted were the crucial facts: Their new coins and tokens were *not* decentralized (and therefore neither immutable nor censorship-resistant), did not have a fair distribution, and so on. What most people still don't get is that if Bitcoin doesn't work, nothing will. This is humanity's best shot at sound money. It is also, very likely, our *only* shot at it.

Many venture capital firms, hedge funds, and retail investors were bamboozled by the buzzword frenzy and invested great sums in these quack-tokens. This generated confusion in the market as many altcoins increased dramatically in price at an even higher rate than Bitcoin. Due to human nature and a lack of understanding basic monetary economics, the bubble grew bigger and bigger, until it inevitably popped and wiped out most of the useless *alternative cryptocurrencies*. Bitcoin experienced ups and downs as well, but they were less volatile. Bitcoin bottomed at levels well above the beginning of the previous bull run and then resumed rising just as it has done several times before. The victims of the altcoin craze will take note of this. They *will* learn the hard way what separates the original from the copycat. They *will* see the undisputable superiority of sound money. It's just a matter of time. Time, which *is* money.

Every time the people of Venezuela, Turkey, Argentina or Zimbabwe are screwed over by their respective central banking authorities and turn to Bitcoin to preserve their savings or income from rampant inflation, the world becomes more aware of Bitcoin as a store of value. In comparison to the Venezuelan Bolivar, there was no crash in Bitcoin at all. There's also a good chance the really big players will accumulate aggressively during the next bull market, given that Bitcoin for the moment still represents a very small allocation of institutional and hedge fund investment. Consider what will happen when institutional investors and a growing number of larger nations start to see Bitcoin's potentially limitless upside. At this point, central banks *will* start to accumulate bitcoins in an attempt to keep up with reality. This will legitimise the technology even further.

It is still unclear *when* this will all play out. When it does, however, it will be the largest transfer of wealth from one medium to another in human history. Early investors, many of which are technically competent, will become financially independent and therefore able to contribute to the ecosystem full-time. More and more people will demand payment in Bitcoin for its ability to store value. Remember that the next block reward halving is just around the corner and that Bitcoin will have an even greater stock-to-flow ratio than gold in just a few years. After the halving in 2020, Bitcoin will have a supply inflation rate of approximately 1.8%, which is lower than the US Federal Reserve's target 2% price inflation rate. It is important to remember that Bitcoin is still an experiment. Should the experiment work, however, hyperbitcoinisation is just a matter of time.

The implications of giving everyone on Earth the ability to rot-proof the fruit of their labour and transport its value through time are hard to overstate. The closest thing we've had to it historically is gold, but gold is not very divisible and not very easy for the general public to get their hands on. More importantly, gold is not *absolutely* scarce. No one knows how much of it there is left buried in the Earth's crust. Investing in real estate has also been seen as a good store of value throughout the ages, but real estate needs a lot of maintenance and is not cheap to hold on to. Real estate is also relatively easy to confiscate in the event of political collapse. Bitcoin provides us with the potential ability to store any amount in our heads and pass it down through generations without anyone ever knowing we had it in the first place. It effectively endows each individual with the power possessed by the feudal kings to turn people into knights. Any Bitcoiner can now dub any no-coiner into a fully fledged time-proof Bitcoiner.

# CHAPTER EIGHT
# CHANGING THE RULES

Altering the Bitcoin protocol is easy. The code is open source which means that anyone can download a copy of the code and make whatever changes they want to it. Altering what the participants of the Bitcoin network view as the real deal, however, is hard. Really hard. Gaining their acceptance requires the proposed upgrade to be really good, and really bulletproof, in terms of not altering the game-theoretical fundamentals that make following the rules beneficial to the miners. Upgrades to the protocol can be implemented via either a soft fork or a hard fork. A *soft fork* is a voluntary, backwards-compatible upgrade. A *hard fork* requires every node in the network that wants to stay active to upgrade its software. At this point in time, it is unlikely that Bitcoin will ever hard fork again. Even a soft fork can be very controversial, and a great debate between proponents of different paths to scaling up the Bitcoin network in 2017 led to a portion of the network "forking off" and creating a new chain via a hard fork. Even though the proposed upgrade was implemented following the consensus rules, some participants weren't very happy with it.

The internet is an ocean of misinformation, and more often than not it is very difficult to navigate through it. The sheer amount of dishonesty in the so-called crypto-space is really depressing and has very little, if anything, to do with sound money. The block chain does one thing and one thing only: It solves the *Byzantine Generals Problem* with the help of Bitcoin's consensus rules. That's it. A problem most people have never even heard of. The Byzantine Generals Problem describes how hard it is to construct a network where the participants can come to a consensus on the true state of the network without needing to know or trust any of the other participants. In other words—how to construct a network in such a way that no trust is required, while ensuring that information sent via the network is true. A block chain by itself does not ensure decentralization. It is not the "underlying technology" behind Bitcoin in any way. Bitcoin is the underlying technology behind the block chain hype, but saying that the block chain is the key invention here is misguided at best. The anchor chain is not the underlying technology behind the anchor. Nor is the keychain the technology behind the key or the food chain the underlying, most interesting aspect of a human being. Be very skeptical of those promoting block chains that do not see Bitcoin's block chain as the most important one. Even social networks with billions of users. They are practically saying that masturbation is the most important aspect of sex.

At any point in time, any participant in the Bitcoin network can stop agreeing with the network's way of determining scarcity and coming to consensus. A participant can choose to follow a hard fork of Bitcoin, exchange all of their bitcoins for another cryptocurrency, or abandon the idea of digital scarcity altogether, if they so choose. What they can't do is change Bitcoin, change what others perceive to be Bitcoin, or change the nature of how Bitcoiners determine scarcity. Unlike every government-backed currency, no one is forcing anyone to agree with anything in Bitcoin. It is a completely voluntary system with no formal leaders. We humans aren't used to leaderless systems, and the idea of having no authority telling us how to think about it is scary to a lot of people. As mentioned above, many opportunists take advantage of this and many people will lose money to scammers before Bitcoin finds its rightful place in our society. Stay vigilant and be suspicious of any "cryptocurrency" that isn't Bitcoin. Every claim that an alternative currency has a new feature, is better for the environment, is faster or more anonymous than Bitcoin, or can be used as a base layer for building decentralized applications, is a testament to misunderstanding what the invention of Bitcoin really was. It was not so much an invention at all but rather a discovery. The discovery of true digital absolute scarcity. Absolute scarcity whose most obvious use case was sound money. A discovery is a one-way occurrence. Thousands of people fly from Europe to America every day, but that doesn't make those people as historically significant as Christopher Columbus. Nor will any social network coin, petro-dollar or altcoin ever be as significant as Bitcoin.

While changing Bitcoin might be really hard, changing the current political state of the world is nearly impossible. Not because of the risk of having your voice drowned out—everyone on the internet faces that hurdle—but because the game is rigged. It's rigged everywhere. Ignorant bloggers with hubris and a paycheck, often referred to as "journalists", often parrot their unseen masters, the central bankers, and accuse Bitcoin of being the biggest pyramid scheme ever known to man. Our current monetary system is a pyramid scheme of such gargantuan proportions that almost everyone on Earth fails to see it for what it is, since the bubble encapsulates the entire planet. Quantitative easing is counterfeiting and counterfeiting is theft. Wealth is stolen from everyone and given to those most cynical and evil among us. If we had sound money, the playing field would be levelled and those of us making the most responsible investments would be rewarded. Right now our system rewards ignorant demagogues and outright liars instead. A hierarchical system of power will always favor those who crave power above all else. A decentralized system will not. It *can* not. It's *fair*.

According to a recent study in the journal *Intelligence*, highly intelligent people are more likely to be diagnosed with various mental disorders such as autism spectrum disorders (20% more likely), ADHD (80%), anxiety (83%) and they have a 182% higher likelihood of suffering from one or more mood disorders. The study compared data from the American Mensa Society to data from national surveys in general. According to another study published a couple of years back in the *British Journal of Psychology*, highly intelligent people are more likely to have fewer friends than those less fortunate in the cognitive department. In addition to this, many separate studies show that ADHD-brains are linked to higher performance in some measures of creativity than their "normal" counterparts.

Having suspected that having a brain "on the spectrum" runs in my family, both up and down the generations, I dug a little deeper into the subject. I did this mainly because I'm curious about myself and why I function the way I function, but also because of the fact that these "diseases" were almost unheard-of when I grew up. I've done a couple of tests online. They all say I'm quite likely to suffer from one of these conditions, mainly ADD. I've heard preschool teachers voice suspicions about spectrum disorders in one of my kids, and even though I suspect that some teachers look a little harder for these things than they probably should, I wouldn't be surprised if the child's behaviour matched more than one of the spectrum-condition criteria. A thing that did surprise me though, was that the Swedish Ministry of Education recently decided to pay extra attention to extraordinarily gifted children. Very un-social-democratic indeed and probably a sound thought. I became curious and looked at the paper on what behaviours teachers should look for in these children. They were remarkably similar to those who could label another child with ADHD or ADD. So, one child gets to skip a class and another is given amphetamine to be more like the rest of the flock, all depending on the judgement of that particular child's teacher.

Ritalin and other amphetamine-like drugs have for a long time been prescribed en masse to children with suspected ADHD and ADD in western societies. Some countries are more restrictive than others, but these practices are present to some extent almost everywhere. People are being given anti-depressants all over the world and there's an opioid epidemic in the United States. Could it be that we're seeing this from the wrong perspective? What do the institutions and schools have to do with our recent love for mental medication? Here's a scary thought: Are we medicating the wrong segment of the population? Could it be that the less intelligent are unable to understand the behaviour of the more intelligent? I'm not saying that everyone "on the spectrum" is hyper-intelligent, but maybe there's a grain of truth here. Not being able to properly adjust to groups may just be a side effect of preferring to be alone. Not being good at submitting to the will of authorities may be a sign of independence rather than simple disobedience. Imagine if Nikola Tesla or Albert Einstein had been given Ritalin at an early age. Would they ever have come up with the amazing innovations and insights that they did if they'd been medicated into being docile sheep instead? Without the crazy ideas of Tesla, who allegedly was considered a weird loner by his peers, we might not have alternating current, without which the world would be a very different and darker place than it is today. Good ideas propel humanity forward and we have no idea what we're missing out on by turning our would-be future inventors and scientists into zombies instead. Keeping the ducks in line might seem beneficial to the collective, but it is only the individual that can spawn an original idea.

Our societies are built upon institutions, and institutions, once in place, have a tendency to act in their own best interest. The people in them have much to lose by not giving in to the will of the machine, so to speak. This includes our schools in which the children are lumped together for many years with potentially nothing in common but their age. They are then forced to imbibe a curriculum adapted to the median, neatly packed into different subjects, and are then graded by the person most likely to be biased against their talent that exists - the teacher. The internet has long since rendered this system obsolete but it seems only free thinkers understand that. If anyone should be medicated, it is not the children "on the spectrum." Instead of giving these kids mind-numbing drugs, maybe we should try giving everyone else mind-enhancing drugs instead? The sad story about dumbing-down the gifted for the sake of the collective is nothing new. The Arab world, for instance, thrived scientifically between the 8th and the 14th century until the collective interest of religion effectively killed that. Socialist states keep collapsing, Venezuela being the latest tragic addition to this collective madness. Russia threw one of their best thinkers ever, Garry Kasparov, in jail. In short, any society that puts the collective before the individual is on a very dangerous path. Thanks to Keynesian economic theory and central bank counterfeiting, or quantitative easing, *all* countries are on this path right now. What are the odds that Satoshi was on Ritalin when he wrote the Bitcoin whitepaper?

Changing the rules of any game is always hard when you're a participant rather than a game designer. The game you're in is rigged and you're a pawn on someone else's chess board. A pawn whose main purpose is to be sacrificed in order to protect the king. Now look at how the artificial intelligence algorithm AlphaZero plays chess. The newly crowned ultimate chess player does one specific move a lot more often than any of its predecessors. It sacrifices pawns. Ask yourself, are you happy with being a pawn? Does your government's promise of a social safety net seem legitimate to you? Will your current job even exist in twenty years? In ten? You don't need to be a pawn. More importantly, you don't need to leave the game entirely. Even a very small investment in Bitcoin has an enormous potential upside. The *Lightning Network* is a technology that changes the rules of what money is and what money can be. Once you have a Lightning Network wallet installed and topped up with some bitcoins on your phone, you quickly realise that it's even easier to use the Lightning Network than it is to use the basic Bitcoin Network. You scan a QR-code and press send. That's it. Transactions on the Lightning Network are instant, free and anonymous. Even though it's still in beta at the time of writing, it works like a dream. Imagine what you can build when money can flow through pipes like water, or even energy. Circuits that run on value instead of electricity. Logic gates made *electronics* possible rather than mere *electrics*. "Value gates" would open up a whole new spectrum of invention, where human interaction would act as fuel for human ingenuity directly.

# CHAPTER NINE
# MONEY AS AN AMPLIFIER

Money can be viewed as many things. It is often described as a *medium of exchange*, a *store of value* and a *unit of account*. As discussed earlier, one can boil down the definition even further. At its very core, money can be defined as a linguistic tool for expressing value, or even just gratitude, to another person, through space and time. From this perspective, money acts as an amplifier of a person's personality. If you're altruistic by nature, suddenly having lots of money won't make you less generous, but rather enable you to express your personality in more ways. Unfortunately, in a cultural environment such as the one we live in now, credit is cheap and economic incentives are skewed. Impulsive, irrational financial decisions in all segments of society are dictating all of our lives. If we didn't have inflation—in other words, if we had sound money—we would be incentivised to save rather than spend. Sustainability would come naturally to us. The lack of sound money also affects the impact money has on our personalities, and its effectiveness as a personality amplifier. Sound money would allow for more honesty and more real solutions to more real problems.

One of the problems that arises from speaking a malfunctioning language of value is that it affects freedom of speech. If the system is rigged to focus on everything but the underlying problem, the entire political landscape becomes a cosmetic charade to keep us from asking the really hard questions about how a human society really ought to operate. Can a person be truly honest publicly in an environment that constantly forces him or her to work harder and harder to afford higher and higher cost of living due to artificial inflation? Those that are wealthy enough might, but the system keeps funneling power from the common person to the elite. In an era where a handful of companies handles almost all internet traffic, subverting free thought can be a very dangerous thing. In addition to the subtle subversion originating from a flawed monetary policy, the titans of Silicon Valley seem more and more prone to give in to the angry mob that proclaim to stand united under the banner of social justice. Political correctness, feeding on a collective feeling of guilt in some parts of the western world, plays a large part in the wave of censorship that has been "de-platforming" some of the more controversial content creators lately.

We live in dangerous times when it comes to freedom of thought. The old media publishers keep claiming that their world view is the only honest one while regular people, and all their different opinions, are increasingly challenging what is and what isn't to be considered as news. The increasing distrust of politicians all over the globe might be a product of fear-mongers to some extent, but it is also a direct consequence of the fact that people have more options when it comes to how they consume information about the current state of the world. In other words, brainwashing is not as easy as it used to be. Unfortunately, distrust in politicians has mostly led to more extreme variations of the same thing. Nationalism on the right and socialism on the left are ideologies on the rise on both sides of the Atlantic. These are red herrings at best. Politicians won't give power back to the people; that's just not what they do. In the next decade, many of humanity's most important decisions will be made. The fate and future of the EU, China and the US will be determined by these decisions. You won't be able to alter or even influence them but you will be able to choose to what extent they will dictate your future. There are ways of opting out of everything. You can quit watching TV, stop reading newspapers, and fill your roof with solar panels but most importantly, you can opt out of the financial system to whatever extent that suits you. Bitcoin is a voluntary system; democracy isn't.

2018 saw the rise of the so-called *intellectual dark web*. An umbrella term for a collection of free thinkers who have used the internet to defend their respective positions in a variety of matters, and freedom of speech particularly, for the last couple of years. Being concerned with the rising trend of de-platforming and censorship on major social media, some of the more popular members of the group are now trying to find alternative ways of monetising their content. Ten years after Bitcoin's immaculate conception, major renegade thinkers are starting to oppose the Orwellian tendencies of the Silicon Valley giants. All the tools we need for taking a stance against censorship are at our disposal, but it's up to each and everyone of us if we dare to use them or not. The internet keeps on disrupting every imaginable business model and shows no signs of slowing down this process. On the contrary, peer-to-peer solutions like Uber and AirBnb are increasingly taking over and exposing "regulated markets" for what they truly are: Cartels. In an era where credit card companies have the power to disconnect any user with an unwanted spending pattern from their money, centralised databases can be very dangerous and a business model is not really disrupted until every rent-seeking middle man has been removed from the equation. Whoever controls the money supply is the ultimate middle man. That's where the cord needs to be cut if we truly want to emancipate ourselves. You decide. Not them. You.

The phenomenon of *fake news* is easier to understand if you remember how much bigger newspaper organisations used to be in the past and what made them smaller. Their whole revenue model was disrupted when the internet turned the advertising industry on its head. All of a sudden, ads were no longer a guessing game, but a precise tool that could be used to collect vast amounts of data about how many potential customers a product would have, and later on, specific data about each and every customer. This led to a downsizing of the news organizations as their ad revenues started to shrink. Simultaneously, everyone on Earth was given the ability to post whatever they had to say to everyone else and to monetise their voices through ads. Both the old and the new media quickly started to accuse each other of spreading false information and the trust that we had all outsourced to journalists, started to erode. Nowadays it's harder than ever to separate trustworthy sources from untrustworthy ones. On the other hand, propaganda machines are harder to build, since everyone's able to hear different perspectives on every subject. What would happen if money itself was to be disrupted in the same way that the old media houses were? What if people started to label "the full faith and credit of the national bank of nation x" as fake news? What happens when we collectively start to question the credibility of our Dollar bills or Euros or Yen? We're about to find out and we can still choose what side of history we want to be on. It's hard to separate real from fake when it comes to news but when it comes to money itself, the perfect tool for evaluating the realness of it, is already there. The market will tell you what's valuable and what's not. Over time, the truth will reveal itself.

Money is an amplifier of ideas and money doesn't really care if the idea itself is good or bad. Political ideas often have the opposite effect of what their intended, or at least advertised, effect is. An income tax for instance, stops generating revenue for the state as soon as the tipping point of the *Laffer curve* is reached. After a certain level, the income tax just prevents people from working altogether. Especially if there's a social insurance policy in place. The Robin Hood -esque narrative of the left is often portrayed as a morally noble thing by its proponents despite the growing number of examples of the opposite all over the globe. The internet startups are leaving San Francisco for Texas and the misfits start flocking in instead. People are literally dying from drug overdoses on the streets while the politically correct overpaid hipster in the neighbouring café enjoys the feeling of superiority that comes with the environmentally friendly paper straw he just got in his chai latte. Opportunist men in their thirties claim to be refugee children in order to leech on the welfare states of Sweden and Germany, creating a political divide and a much worse situation for those in actual need of help. In a world with *sound money*, the greedy would have to provide a lot more value to their fellow man in order to accumulate wealth since money would be harder to come by. We'd better remember that Robin Hood was first and foremost fighting *against* taxes. Money is an amplifier and unsound money inevitably produces unsound societies.

As the Bitcoin network grows, so does its fee market. Some people argue that because of this, Bitcoin cannot scale. This viewpoint stems from an unsound attitude towards Bitcoin. Some loud-mouthed actors in the cryptocurrency community start to bicker and moan whenever Bitcoin chooses to implement or, more often than not, chooses to *not* implement a proposed upgrade. Their view of what Bitcoin ought to be doesn't matter to Bitcoin. Bitcoin's ironclad resistance to the whims of the self-entitled early investor Tony Stark wannabes of its social media entourage is one of the biggest aspects of what makes it so special. Imagine trying to buy a cup of coffee with gold. In order to make a safe transaction, where the validity of your tiny gold pebble was verified by several independent chemists and your pebble was transported to your local Starbucks in an armored van, you would have to pay an absolutely enormous "fee". Despite its obvious flaws as a *medium of exchange*, gold is very valuable. Despite its complicated divisibility, its lack of eligible usage properties, its lack of a decentralized Layer 2 scaling solution and its relatively easy confiscatability, gold remains a good *store of value*. Bitcoin is also, regardless of what anyone thinks about it, a *store of value* above a *medium of exchange*. This is more important than it might seem. If bitcoin should fail at holding value long term, its whole value proposition would disappear. A fast and smooth, highly centralized *medium of exchange* is not a groundbreaking invention in any sense. We already have plenty of those. It is quite arrogant to think that your own personal influence could steer Bitcoin in another direction. You can deceive people into thinking that your fork of Bitcoin is the real deal, but that will damage your reputation more than it will damage Bitcoin in the long run. A fork of Bitcoin ignores Bitcoin's consensus rules and that makes a fork little more than any other copy-pasted code.

Admitting that you're a Bitcoiner publically is not without risk. Not only does it pose a personal risk to you as you become a potential target for burglars and thieves, but in doing so you also put your reputation at stake. Not mainly because of the reason people think, namely that bitcoin might not work and its price might go to zero because of this or that. The biggest damage to the reputation of us Bitcoiners is being done by the seemingly endless amount of scammers and free-riders that this technology attracts. Even though the Bitcoin network is a lot bigger than any of its competitor's networks, people outside of the cryptocurrency space are having a hard time telling the difference. As most (if not all) of bitcoin's rivals are scams, bitcoin is being perceived as guilty by association by a large portion of the general public. This may cause the public Bitcoin enthusiast a lot of reputational damage short term. Long term however, is a different matter altogether. Long term, denying the impact bitcoin will have might be a far worse opinion to hold. The people going public with their ill-informed skepticism to something they don't fully understand will be remembered in the same manner as those comparing the internet to a fancy fax-machine in the nineties. Bitcoin is hard to understand because it shatters many political ideas since money becomes virtually non confiscatable in a bitcoin dominated world economy. Just as the business models of the twentieth century that revolved around charging people for selling them copies of films, music or books got shattered by subscription services such as Netflix,

Spotify or Audible, macroeconomic business models based on the notion that you can force people to crowdfund projects through taxes or inflation will suffer the same fate if they don't adapt quickly enough. This realization is way too big a mental somersault for some people to grasp. It turns how we think about value on its head and forces us to accept the hard truths of economics, currently only truly understood by economists of the Austrian variety. Given a generation or two though, Bitcoin's advantages will simply be undeniable.

# CHAPTER TEN
# THE ENVIRONMENT

There's no such thing as a free lunch. There's no such thing as a zero sum game. The 2nd law of thermodynamics tells us this. You know, the one about entropy and how everything will be really lame in a couple of trillion years. There's no action without an equally big reaction somewhere. This is also true for bitcoin mining. Every once in a while, some ignorant clickbait hungry journalist writes an article about Bitcoin's energy usage and how it's connected to global warming or how widespread bitcoin adoption would kill us all someday because of its "wasteful" production process. What they all fail to address is the alternative cost. As mentioned before, bitcoins are valuable because they're scarce and they're scarce *because* they're costly to produce. The same is true for gold or diamonds or anything else that is scarce and hard to come by. As discussed in earlier chapters, the mining algorithm can never be any more energy efficient because the electricity spent is directly linked to the value of the token.

Secondly, think about what most people use their bitcoins for. Nothing. That's right, nothing. Bitcoin incentivizes saving rather than spending. This is the exact opposite of how people use money in our current system of fiat currencies, because bitcoin is deflationary rather than inflationary, relative to all other currencies. This means that every Dollar, Yen or Pound spent on bitcoins would have ended up being spent on some other energy demanding thing, had it not been spent on the bitcoins. Either that or it would have lost its value due to inflation which implies that even more Dollars, Yen or Euros would have been created, and spent on frivolous things. Right now, credit is cheap and the underlying economic theory of our time is based on the idea that the amount of *spending* going on in society is a key metric in economics. Bitcoin, on the other hand, is based on the economic theories of the *Austrian school*, where *saving* is the key metric. Yes, they're costly to produce, but so is overproducing every product on Earth because every business needs to expand as fast as possible to pay off their loans. Human well being has always, and will always be, linearly connected to energy consumption. You can't get around, or bypass this fact. Energy consumption and human flourishing, are inevitably linked. The thing bitcoin does, is to take away the need for unnecessary energy consumption by incentivizing us to save for future generations. It's a mechanism that hinders our self-destructive tendencies. Not a threat to our planet's health, but a remedy.

The next time you hear about the Bitcoin network using as much energy as a small country, ask yourself - where would all that energy have ended up if it wasn't funneled into the only invention trying to save us from ourselves there is? Into a Chinese factory producing consumer goods shipped by boat, truck and car for temporary use and probably ending up in a garbage pile the size of a small country in less than a year? How is that better for the planet? The only place solutions for humanity's problems can stem from, is from human ingenuity. Such ingenuity in turn, stems from places where people with brains have a shot at getting somewhere in life. Thanks to the internet and bitcoin, that somewhere is everywhere. The internet connects us, and bitcoin frees up our time and emancipates us from our current, destructive systems. Bitcoin helps you plant a seed and watch it grow. Before you criticize bitcoin, try to comprehend *why* it was invented and what inflationary, soft money does to the mechanisms of the market. Try to understand why we have a "climate problem" in the first place. Why we over consume. What underlying forces pull our psychological strings and make us lend money for a new car? It takes a special kind of ignorance to criticize a solution without first fully comprehending the problem.

There's one specific word that describes the current global environmentalist movement better than any other and that is "hubris". Yes, the Earth has been getting warmer, very slowly, over the last fifty years. Yes, at least one of the ice caps might be melting. Yes, it's probably because of human activity but no, you can't save the planet through political interference in people's lives. To get every nation on Earth to agree that it is a good idea to forcefully make people change their behaviour for the sake of the climate, is not only impossible, but also cruel and counter productive. Collectivists always disguise their urge to deprive their fellow man of his or her possessions and freedoms as a necessary thing to do, in order to "save" humanity. This is nothing new. They've just decided that "climate change" is the most effective banner to rally under right now. The causes change, but the underlying philosophy stays the same. It's very disturbing that the socialist experiment gets to repeat itself so many times in so many parts of the world.

Human progress and human flourishing have linear relationships to energy usage. If we want to find new ways of bettering ourselves we should use *more* energy, not less. Truly free market competition leads to the most efficient solutions and there are a bunch of incentives for producers of consumable goods to find cheap energy sources. Bitcoin provides the market with yet another incentive. To find locations for, and investing in, power plants in remote areas of the world where the cost barrier for building the plant has been too high historically, due to the costly and wasteful process of transporting electricity. Hydro-electric plants in areas with a high risk of flooding, for instance. These areas are not suitable for human settlements, but they could provide us with a lot of electricity. When producers have the option to convert electricity into money directly, they're *more* likely to use renewable energy sources, not less. In this sense, bitcoin can function as a battery for energy producers.

Offshore wind farms have a very specific wind force range where they produce a usable amount of electricity. The bigger the turbine the wider the range, but they still have an upper and a lower windforce limit. If an offshore wind farm was connected to a bitcoin mining rig, the surplus energy produced on windy days could have been converted into a profit for the producer instantly. The same logic applies to solar farms and geothermal plants. Energy is not a finite resource in any practical sense for the inhabitants of Mother Earth. If we could harness and store all the power of all the sunlight that hits the Earth during just one day, we could satisfy all of humanity's energy needs for a couple of hundred years. Bitcoin's role in all of this is unexplored, but its potential to be a very positive environmental force is huge, and it will prove its utility during the next century. On one hand it provides energy producers with a battery, on the other hand it gives central bankers a run for their money and ultimately forcing them to adopt a more sound monetary policy or become obsolete altogether. Bitcoin creates an incentive for sacrificing surplus energy for a small profit and a greater good rather than just letting it go to waste. The energy harnessed is converted into a completely scarce asset which is divisible and transportable to a much greater extent than any other valuable resource on Earth. It incentivizes the energy producer to think long term and will reward those most patient and least wasteful among them. This recalibration of incentive structures is of course not only limited to energy producers or miners, but to anyone who embraces this technology and understands its implications. In due time, bitcoin's superior monetary properties will be undeniable to even the most stubborn dinosaur. This would be an enormous net gain for humanity *and* the environment.

Courageous politicians dare to implement unpopular policies. They don't need climate striking teenagers to tell them which issues ought to be addressed first. It is ironic how celebrities that score cheap points by talking about the climate, often accuse their political opponents of being "populist". What *really* happens when you raise carbon taxes and try to force populations into behaviours that they don't really like? The *gilets jaunes*, or yellow vests, in France are a great example. People still have to commute to work. Raising taxes solves nothing, it just distorts the market and relocates the problem. The only thing the recently adopted environmentalist policies of France resulted in was the destruction of Paris. Arguably not the best thing for the environment. In a truly free society, a society with *sound money*, climate-striking children wouldn't be a problem. They would have to learn to cooperate in order to address whatever imaginary problem they sought to solve which would be harmless to the rest of us. Now, when backed by fear-mongering journalists, they can cause a ton of damage as our virtue-signalling political class needs to adapt to whatever imaginary issue the press has primed us with in order to secure votes. It's not about whether there is a real climate problem or not, but rather about motives. Always ask yourself, what does this person stand to gain from holding this particular opinion? Can this issue *really* be solved by political means?

## Sovereignty Through Mathematics

There's no such thing as a free lunch. There *is* such a thing as *representation* however, and there's *always* a personal economic motive behind political decisions. They're not here for you, you're here for them. One of the most eye-opening experiences of my life was seeing the lobbyist quarters in Brussels. The rise of veganism, placebic gluten-intolerance and meat-free mondays in school cafeterias are all products of the food industry. A soy burger is a lot cheaper to produce than a beef one. To anyone that can sell it at a higher price by appealing to people's vanity or world-saving hubris, huge profits await. They've managed to monetise our collective bad climate-conscience in such a cunning way that most of us have no clue we're being played. In the 20th century, the cereal-killers of the Kellogs company and their likes funded "research" that cemented a fear of red meats and saturated fats into the minds of the public. The effects of this propaganda can very much still be seen today as the inhabitants of America are about twice as fat today than they were before the introduction of "light" products to the market. All of these things are connected to the root of the problem, the lack of *sound money*. Inflation made it possible for the food industry to replace our homemade beef burger with a mass-produced cheap soy substitute while making us believe that the price of a burger hadn't changed that much the last fifty years. Spoiler alert - it had.

Another of the most eye-opening experiences I've had was during my stay in a Mayan village in the Toledo district of Belize about ten years ago. I spent a couple of days with a family of two adults and six children in a jungle village of huts and no electricity save for two diesel generators. One night, the father of the house told me a story about his friend going into politics a decade earlier and being murdered for having the wrong opinions. We slept on wooden beds without mattresses and a couple of dogs and turkeys ran freely around the village. One day, the family's ten year old was listening to some Bob Marley songs on a CD-player connected to a car battery and a small solar panel on a pole in the garden. I listened for a while and then asked him about the strange sound effects in between the songs. Helicopter sounds, machine gun sounds and other strange noises were intersecting the songs here and there. He replied by telling me that "...oh, it's not a proper CD, I made it with Virtual DJ on my cousin's laptop". I was stunned. Here was this ten year old, in the middle of the jungle, being just as skilled with a computer as any other ten year old I ever met. In that moment, I realised just how levelled the playing field has been for the workforce across the globe. Here was this child, living in a hut without even electricity but without a mortgage to inherit, ready to compete on the same global market as any other kid in the world. Bitcoin is the logical next step. Bitcoin doesn't care about nationality, gender, ethnicity, age, sexual preferences or any other imagined victimization or privilege. To Bitcoin, we're all equal. It is a voluntary system and it knows no biases. Bitcoin is *equality of opportunity* in its purest form and it doesn't have any opinion on outcome whatsoever.

## CHAPTER ELEVEN
## A NEW FORM OF LIFE

It's not easy to define the properties that would deem an entity a new form of life. There's no consensus among scientists, nor nations, regarding the definition of what a life form is. This is one of the main hurdles when it comes to defining artificial or synthetic life. How does one know when life has been created, if there's no clear definition of what life actually is? One popular definition of life is that a living organism is an open system that maintains homeostasis, is composed of cells, has a life cycle, undergoes metabolism, can grow, adapt to its environment, respond to stimuli, reproduce and evolve. Could Bitcoin fit into this description? In order to find out, we need to dissect both this definition of life and the basic properties of the Bitcoin network. Bitcoin is quite clearly an open system but what does it mean for an organism to *maintain homeostasis*? Homeostasis is the tendency towards a relatively stable equilibrium between interdependent elements, especially (but not limited to) as maintained by physiological processes. The first part of that sentence perfectly describes what Bitcoin does. The *equilibrium* is the *consensus* between the *nodes,* which act as *interdependent elements.* One could even argue that they actually are *maintained by physiological processes,* since each node's decisions are ultimately made by human brains and not software, but for now, we'll examine Bitcoin as a life form from a non-meta-argument perspective. The next part of the definition is that life is made up of cells which the Bitcoin network also arguably is, especially if you count *nodes* as cells.

A life cycle is defined as a "series of changes in form that an organism undergoes, returning to the starting state", according to Wikipedia. The life cycle of the Bitcoin network is still unclear, but it seems unlikely that it would ever return to its starting state. What is more likely is that while we have witnessed its birth, it is highly unlikely that any human alive today will outlive the network, so we won't have any way of knowing. This is not unheard of in nature either however. A species of fungi called *Armillaria Ostoyae*, or the *Humongous Fungus*, in the Blue Mountains of Oregon, is one of the largest and oldest organisms ever known to man. This network of mushroom is estimated to be between 2500 and 8500 years old based on its current growth rate. No one knows what its life cycle looks like in perfect detail. The three main purposes of *metabolism* in a living body are the conversion of food to energy to run cellular processes, the conversion of food into bodily building blocks, and the elimination of nitrogenous wastes. Bitcoin's metabolism works in a similar manner. Bitcoin feeds on electricity and its cellular processes are its transactions. Its body has its own building blocks, literal blocks, that are added to its body, the block chain, roughly every ten minutes. Malicious blocks are considered waste and are thus eliminated by the system. Bitcoin grows and adapts to its environment organically, exemplified lately by the development of the *Lightning Network* and other Layer 2 scaling solutions. It responds to external stimuli by showing a more and more ironclad resistance to change, while still responding well to sufficiently clever improvement proposals. Like the *Armillaria Ostoyae,* Bitcoin rather *grows* than reproduces and it *evolves* over time by adopting good ideas and rejecting bad ones. The notion of Bitcoin as a life form may sound far fetched and even a bit silly, even though a lot of its properties fit the bill. What we *do* know about it is that it is *very* unlikely to go away or stop functioning for any foreseeable future. Whether or not it lives is up for debate, but it can't be killed and that ought to mean something. We should study it carefully and try to be as unbiased and humble as possible when drawing conclusions about it.

Speaking of fungi, one of the most important aspects of money is its *fungibility*. Fungibility goes hand-in-hand with privacy and censorship resistance. If certain Bitcoin addresses were to end up on a government's blacklist, they'd end up becoming less valuable than their not yet blacklisted neighbors. Look at what happened to the Indian Rupee bills that were banned overnight by the Indian government in late 2017 in order to "fight corruption". They're still in use, but only worth about 70% of the value they held when they were considered "legal tender". If bitcoin transactions can't be private, they won't be fungible. This reduces bitcoin's monetary capability. We're at a point in history where bitcoin transactions can be completely private but only a select few people know how to ensure that they really are. This is arguably bitcoin's greatest flaw and a very real hurdle on the way to mainstream adoption.

So how many privacy measures does the average user need to take? Just as when it comes to storage, it depends on the user's knowledge level. Most users should probably be more careful than they are right now, but there's little reason to be paranoid. It's still very hard to prove that a specific transaction was made by a specific user. The whole ordeal is somewhat akin to the fight against the BitTorrent network ten years ago. The copyright lobby found different means of scaring off users in different parts of the world, banning websites, prosecuting providers and so on, but the network itself is still thriving and torrent files are as accessible as they ever were. A lot of heads will probably have to roll before bitcoin is accepted everywhere but just like they couldn't fight filesharing, governments won't be able to fight Bitcoin. Even the policymakers will understand the advantages of bitcoin usage sooner or later. The word *later* is key here. If you want to be absolutely sure that what you do with your bitcoins is legal, private, or worthwhile, just wait. Wait out the storm and don't use them until they're fully acceptable everywhere. They'll be worth a lot more and you'll have a lot more options in general. Remember, HODLing is using.

One of the greatest hidden perks of bitcoin adoption is that it forces people to think for themselves. First, it forces the user to think about computer security. In order to store your bitcoins safely you have to know what you're doing, what software and hardware you can trust etc. It is virtually impossible to do anything online without trusting *any* third party. Every piece of hardware and software inside, and in between, each of the two computers communicating could potentially be corrupt. In Bitcoin, the cautious user will be rewarded and the reckless user will be punished eventually. This is also true for Bitcoin's on- and off ramps and the less cautious user is always more likely to end up in legal trouble. The coming tsunami that is hyperbitcoinisation is scary, but a skilled surfer can expect the ride of his lifetime.

# CHAPTER TWELVE
# THE YEARS AHEAD

The *Lindy effect* is a theory that describes the future life expectancy of a technology or an idea. It states that an idea's expected remaining lifespan is proportional to its current age, so that every additional period of survival implies a longer remaining life expectancy. Bitcoin, which is not only an idea but also a technology and a social experiment, is ten years old now and therefore we can expect it to stay around for at least another ten.

At the time of writing, there are exactly 17,669,941 bitcoins around and twelve and a half new ones are created every ten minutes. 17,669,941 is about 84% of the total supply, i.e. the total number of bitcoins that will ever exist. Ten years from now, around twenty million bitcoins will have been found. Three more block reward halvings will have taken place and the reward for each block found will be 1.5625 bitcoins. The whole world will have a little more than two and a half million new bitcoins around. This is to be compared with the more than seventeen and a half million that was created during the last ten years when they were cheap and relatively easy to come by. In the network's first couple of years you could acquire several bitcoins by just claiming them from special websites called faucets, every once in a while. The Dollar's cumulative rate of inflation was 15.6 percent during this period. This means that each Dollar lost more than one sixth of its value in the last ten years due to quantitative easing, which is the central banker's term for counterfeiting. It is very unlikely that the cumulative rate of inflation for the US Dollar in the upcoming ten years will be any lower than these 15.6 percent, since the fractional reserve lending system requires a little *more* inflation each year to sustain itself. So, a little less than 2.5 million new bitcoins to share and at least 20% more US Dollars in circulation to buy them with.

Now, let's look at the internet itself. *Metcalfe's Law* states that the value of a communications network is proportional to the amount of users on the network squared. Each new internet user is a potential new bitcoin user, especially in those places on the planet where there's poor internet connectivity, because those places often have a weak local currency that bitcoin functions as a hedge against. In 2008, 23% of the world's population had access to the internet and in 2018, that number was 48%. In the developing world the numbers were 14% in 2008 and 41% in 2018. The global numbers might not double again in the forthcoming ten years but it looks like they'll keep on rising, especially in the developing countries, where they might just double again. All of these indicators (fewer bitcoins, more fiat money, more internet users) point toward a rising bitcoin price, regardless of its current valuation. Bitcoin has risen in value extremely fast and has added, on average, an additional zero at the end of its price figure roughly every three years. Can it really keep on doing so? Think about the underlying forces that drive the price up. Every single mobile device could potentially hold bitcoins yet only a select few do. When more and more people embrace the technology, the whole fear of missing out cycle starts again and the price jumps up to the next plateau. Note also that every current bitcoin user can do three things with his or her bitcoins - sell them, lose them or hold them. On top of this, nothing is stopping an existing bitcoin user from acquiring new bitcoin.

Bitcoin is an internet protocol that is very resistant to change. It showed an unprecedented example of this in late 2017 when all of the biggest companies in Bitcoin decided that they were going to implement the proposed Segregated Witness upgrade and then hard fork to 2 megabyte blocks a couple of months later. Segregated Witness, which most users wanted, was activated but the network's users resisted the 2 megabyte block hard fork. This led to a lot of frustration among the proponents of the hard fork and led to the creation of a copycat altcoin called Bitcoin Cash. The Price of both tokens rose quickly in the aftermath of the fork, but in hindsight the event was more of a train robbery than a christmas gift, confusing at best. Segregated Witness does not only free up block space, but it also allows for Layer 2 scaling solutions to be built on top of Bitcoin, such as the Lightning Network. The Lightning network allows for instant, completely anonymous, nearly free micro transactions that do not take up block space and it is up and running right now. In addition to this, the number of Lightning Network transactions that can be carried out simultaneously are only limited by the bandwidth of the nodes. This makes the Lightning Network a future real competitor to Visa or Mastercard. Many other Layer 2 upgrades are in the works but the core Bitcoin network functions the same way it always has with its inputs and outputs, its public and private keys and so on.

Will some other token ever replace bitcoin then? After all, more efficient protocols are out there. Short answer

- no. This has been mentioned several times before in this book but it can't be stressed enough. Scarcity on the internet was a one time discovery. It was a one time invention and it cannot be repeated because resistance to replicability *is* the invention. Bitcoin's history and unique position is what makes it truly scarce and resistant to change and these first ten years will not repeat themselves for any "alternative" token. There is still a lot of confusion about what Bitcoin is, and the idea of sound money on the internet is a hard concept to grasp since humans haven't ever encountered absolute scarcity before. The best path forward for any person is arguably to educate him- or herself and others about the invention and what it means. Time will tell whether your sources were true or false, and it is unlikely that Bitcoin will achieve mass adoption in the next couple of years. Still, the infrastructure is in place and the interfaces of its surrounding software, like wallets, are getting more and more user friendly every day. Remember, the iPhone was first introduced to the world in 2007 and smartphones had enormous corporate marketing to help them succeed, all along the way. Bitcoin grows organically. Let it breathe and watch it evolve but whatever you do, don't miss the opportunity and acquire some while you still can, at this discounted price.

SOVEREIGNTY THROUGH MATHEMATICS

## AFTERTHOUGHT

I hope you've learned something from reading this book and I encourage every reader to fact check me and challenge my opinions. Ideas left unchallenged seldom age well. All opinions, political or not, expressed in the book are first and foremost meant to be thought provoking and are not meant to be taken too literally.

Finally, I recommend reading some of the old Ludwig von Mises. "Human Action", for instance. Perhaps while listening to some of the old Ludwig van Beethoven. The third movement of the "Moonlight Sonata", for instance.

Printed in Great Britain
by Amazon